D0319678

Schools Library and Information Service
*S00000159218*

## Up the Garden Path

For Anna M – J.A.

For Beth, Daz and Tom
and especially for Clair – T.H.



KINGFISHER
Kingfisher Publications Plc
New Penderel House
283–288 High Holborn
London WC1V 7HZ

First published by Kingfisher Publications Plc 2000

2 4 6 8 10 9 7 5 3 1

1TR(1BFC)/0300/TWP/DIG/150NYMA



A CIP catalogue record for this book is available from
the British Library.

ISBN 0 7534 0419 2

Editor: Katie Puckett
Series Designer: Jane Tassie

Additional research: Warren Collum

Printed in Singapore

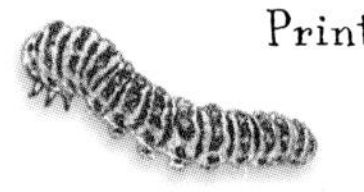

Up the Garden Path

# Are you a Butterfly?

Judy Allen and Tudor Humphries

KINGFISHER

Are you a butterfly?

If you are, your parents look like this.

You start life in an
egg like this.

As soon as you are strong
enough, break out of it.
You do not look like your
mother or father.

You are
a caterpillar.

You have
sixteen legs, a
hairy back with
tiny breathing holes in it,
and very small eyes. You have no
nose, but you do have
a mouth.

So eat.

Eat whatever you are standing on.

Your mother laid your egg on
a delicious leaf.

Grip the leaf with your legs to hold
it steady. Then eat it.

Now eat the next leaf.

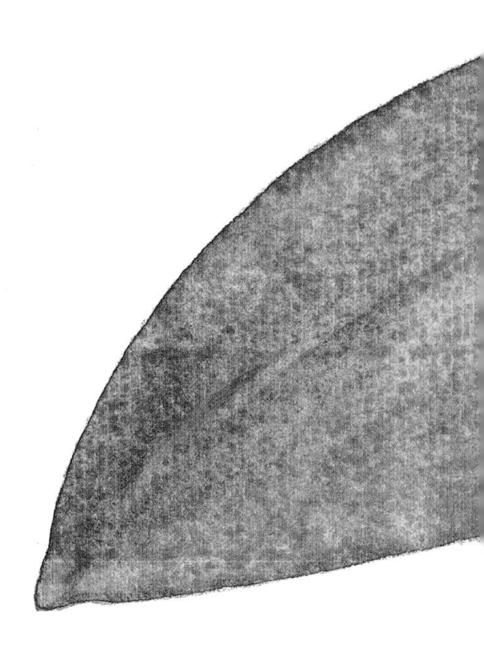

Eat every leaf you can reach.
Then move to the nearest leaves
and eat them too.

Grow **bigger**.

And **bigger**.

Eat more.

You feel full.

You feel so full you think

you are going to burst.

You are right,

you ARE going to burst.

Before you burst,
glue yourself on to
a leaf or a stem so you
won't fall off.

Your skin will split
all the way down
your back.

Don't panic.
This is normal.
Climb out of your old skin.

You may have to wriggle
around a bit
to do this.

As you eat and grow,
you will have to climb out
of your skin two or
three more times.

One day you will feel funny.
It is time to find somewhere safe
and glue yourself on.

You are going to turn into a chrysalis.

You may not be able to spell it,
but you will be able
to do it.

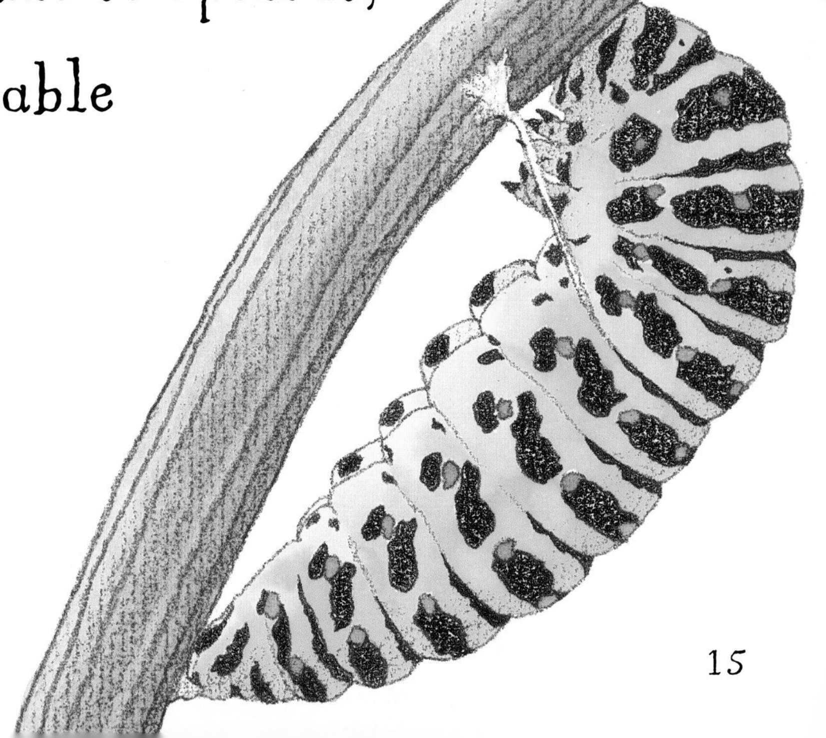

You will change while you are in your chrysalis. You will change a lot.

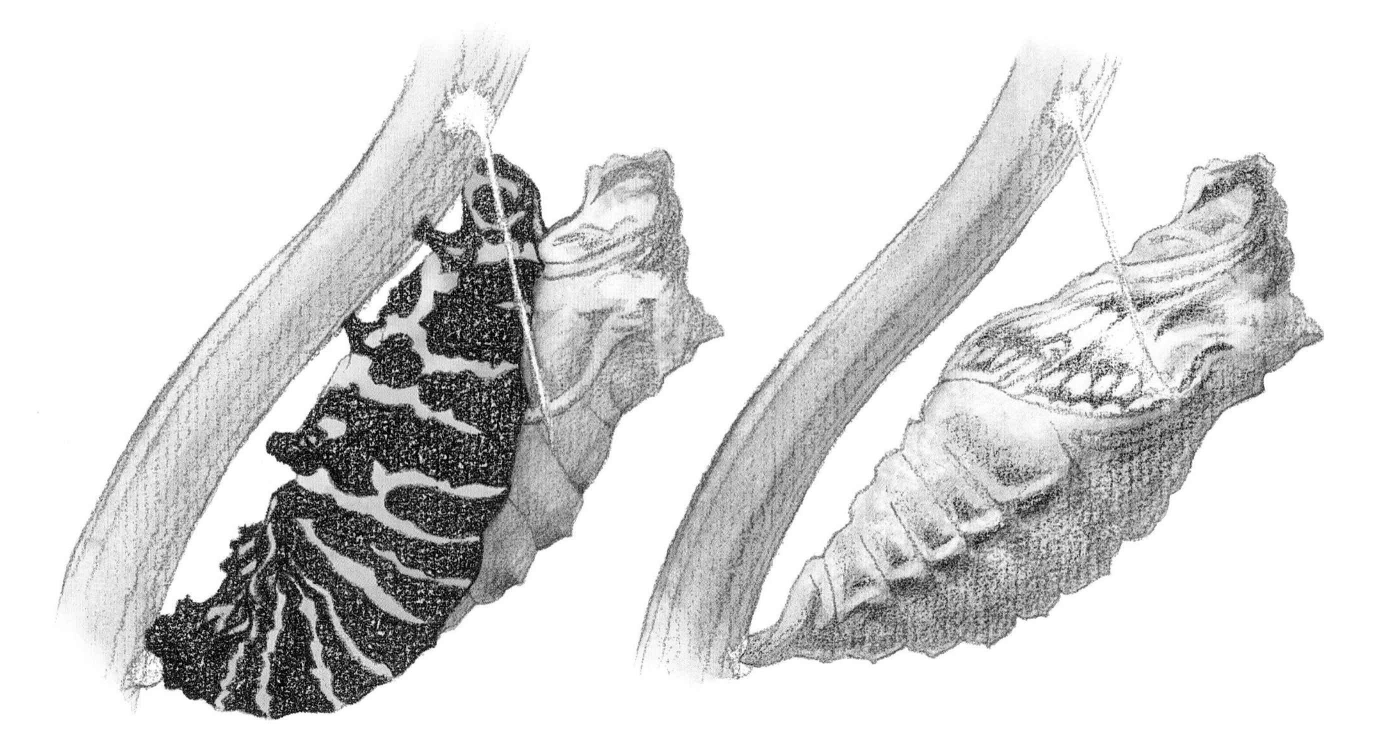

You will grow six legs instead of sixteen. You will grow large eyes instead of small eyes.

You will grow long feelers on your head.
You will grow wings!

When you have done all these things – break out of your chrysalis.

Your wings are crumpled.
They look terrible.

Don't worry. Hang upside down
from your chrysalis.

Slowly, slowly,
your wings will stretch.
The creases will all go.

Use the long feelers on your head to smell flowers.

Use your long tongue to drink nectar from the hearts of flowers.

Use your wings to fly!

Now it is time to look at
a picture of yourself.

If you look a little like this

or this

or this, you are not a butterfly.

You are not even a caterpillar.

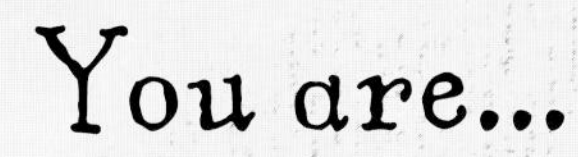


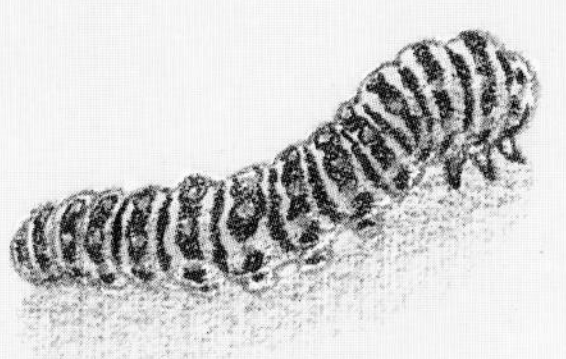

... a human child.

You have no wings.

You can't fly.

It is most unlikely that you have long feelers growing out of the top of your head.

Never mind, you can do a great many things that butterflies can't do.

Also you will never have to turn into a chrysalis.

And you will never,

ever, EVER

have to eat so much your skin splits.

# Did You Know...

...if a human baby grew as fast as a caterpillar it would weigh about 8 tonnes when it was only two weeks old.

...there are about 15,000 different kinds of butterfly in the world.

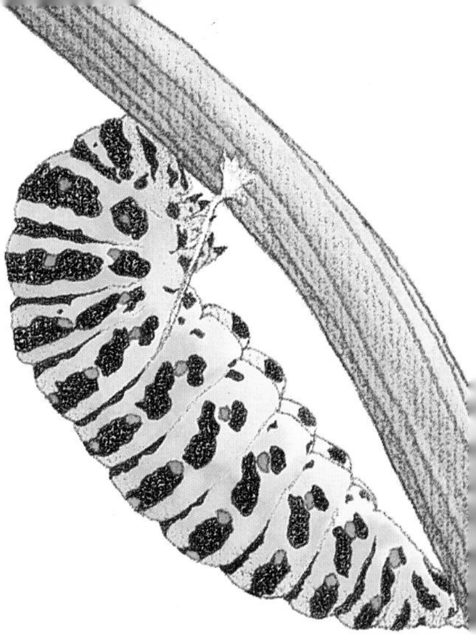

...the Queen Alexandra butterfly of Papua New Guinea is the largest in the world – when its wings are spread out it measures nearly 30 centimetres across.

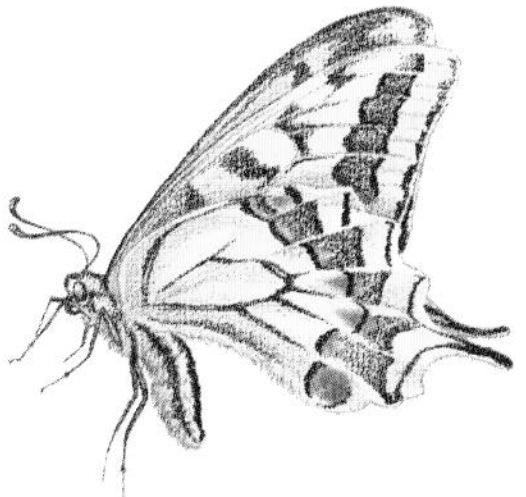

...butterfly wings are covered with thousands of tiny, brightly coloured scales. It's important never to touch a butterfly's wings. They are easily damaged and if the butterfly can't fly any more, it will die.